GW01036186

SLANG DICTIONARY

Frank Povah

VB

ESKY

Editor Averil Moffat
Text Frank Povah
Art Director Mike Ellott
Book design Lucy Charlotte
Illustrations Michael Weldon
Print Production Christopher Clear
Production Editor Jess Teideman
Education Editor Lauren Smith
Proofreader Ken Eastwood

Publishing Director Cornelia Schultz
Publisher Jo Runciman
Editor-in-Chief, Australian Geographic Chrisse Goldrick

Printed in China by Leo Paper Products

First published in 2015 by Bauer Media
54 Park St, Sydney NSW 2000
Telephone: (02) 9263 9813
Email: editorial@ausgeo.com.au
www.australiangeographic.com.au

Australian Geographic customer service:
1300 555 176 (local call rate within Australia)
From overseas +61 2 8667 5295

The Aussie Slang Dictionary

Australian English has always been rich in slang and dialect words, many of which – 'dinkum' for example – came from Great Britain with the convicts and then had their meanings and pronunciation changed. Words from Indigenous languages, such as 'boomerang', began to be adopted and modified almost from the very first – and English words and phrases, such as 'dead finish', were taken into Aboriginal languages, modified and loaned back to the English speakers. As time went by, words still in common use in Australia were no longer current in their country of origin, and so became Australianised.

Australians' excursions abroad to fight for the Empire in colonial wars, in two World Wars and various other conflicts, along with large influxes of immigrants from all over the world, saw words from many other languages added to the rich stew, a stew that still simmers and bubbles with vitality.

Convict beginnings and national experiences of a climate that stubbornly refuses to cooperate have given Australia a unique, if sardonic, sense of humour, and this, too, is reflected in many of the phrases used.

Some of the words listed here are almost obsolete – though an attentive traveller may still hear them in remote places – but have been included to demonstrate the awe-inspiring depth of Aussie English.

HOW TO USE THE AUSSIE SLANG DICTIONARY

Words are organised alphabetically, with phrases and sentences alphabetised according to the subject of the sentence.

Related phrases and words are defined together, shown in a highlighted box.

An asterisk (*) indicates that a word was borrowed from an Indigenous language or from Aboriginal English.

ACT THE GOAT: play the fool

ACTARIAN: resident of the Australian Capital Territory (ACT)

AKUBRA: a brand of felt hat made from wild rabbit fur

ALICE, THE: Alice Springs

ALL THE GO: a la mode, all the rage

ALLIGATOR: sometimes used to describe the 'saltie', the saltwater crocodile

AMBO: ambulance officer, paramedic

ANZAC: member of the Australian and New Zealand Army Corps in WWI; the archetypal

A

Aussie (sometimes used derisively for a show-off, "Coming the big bronzed Anzac")

ANZAC DAY: commemorates the Anzac landing at Gallipoli, see Dawn Service

APPLE ISLANDER: Tasmanian; see *also Taswegian*

ARMPITS LIKE A GREEK WRESTLER'S JOCK STRAP: offensive body odour

ARSE/ARSEY: pure good luck, very lucky

ARSE LIKE A WORKING BULLOCK: extremely wide in the buttocks

ARSE-ABOUT: back to front

ARSE-UP, TO GO: fall over, upside down

ARVO: afternoon

AS FIT AS A MALLEE BULL: very strong

AS USEFUL AS TITS ON A BOAR/BILL: of no use at all

AUSSIE: anything Australian, including its peoples, but never the country

AUSSIE SALUTE: to brush flies from the face

B

AXE, THE (ALSO SACK, BULLET): termination of employment, do away with

AY: an affirmation, also used to add weight to a statement, as "She'll be right, ay!"

B-DOUBLE: a truck consisting of a prime mover with a fixed tray or trailer and a second trailer connected by a fifth wheel

B&S: Bachelor and Spinsters' Ball, infamous annual dances and drinking festivals for young men and women from the country

BACKHANDER: a bribe; an insult

BACK OF BOURKE: anywhere remote

BAG, TO: to demean or belittle someone

BAG SWINGER: a street prostitute

BALLS UP: confusion, a bad mistake (from Australian Rules football)

B

BANANA BENDER: a Queenslander

BANDICOOT: a small animal; to remove something without a trace

BANJO: a shovel

BARBIE: barbecue

BARCOO ROT: a scurvy-like disease

BARDIE: a large, edible wood grub (WA)

BARKING UP THE WRONG TREE: making a mistake

BARNEY: a fight or argument

BARRACK: to urge on, particularly a sports team

BARRACKER: team supporter, fan

B

BASH: to do something purposefully, see *ear-basher, spine-basher*

BASH THE SPINE: a nap, forty winks

BASTARD: almost impossible to define, for its meaning depends not only on context, but on inflection and occasion. 'Lousy bastard', for example, can express admiration for a friend who is a frugal spender, but it can also be a term of derision for an unpopular politician. However, it is rarely used in a derogatory way to describe someone born out of wedlock, for that carries no stigma among ordinary Australians

BASTARDRY: despicable behaviour, particularly in regard to political dealings

BATHERS: swimming costume (mainly in use in WA and Vic.)

BATTLER: Mr or Ms Everyman, Joe

B

Citizen, Jane Doe
BEAK: magistrate
BEANIE: woollen skullcap
BEAUT: something really good
BEAUT UTE: a ute especially tricked out for competitions
BEAUTY (OFTEN PRONOUNCED BEWDY): an expression of approval or delight
BEDOURIE OVEN: a camp oven made of spun steel and less prone to breakage than the

traditional cast iron model
BELL: a telephone call; see *ring*
BERK: a fool

B

BETTER THAN A POKE IN THE EYE WITH A BURNT STICK/BLUNT STICK: better than the alternative, lesser of two evils

BEYOND/OUT PAST THE BLACK STUMP: a mythical landmark beyond which lies the unknown

BICKY/IES: money; a cookie

BIG ISLAND, THE: Tasmanian name for the mainland

BILL THE BULLOCKY: mythical owner of the dog that sits on the tuckerbox; see *dog on the tuckerbox*

BILLABONG: a large pool or pond left by receding floodwaters, a backwater

B

BILLY: tin can with a handle used for making tea on a campfire

BINDI-I*: a ground-hugging prickle

BINJI*: the stomach

BISCUIT: see *bicky*

BITIE: shark

BLACK AS THE EARL OF HELL'S RIDING BOOTS: describing threatening storm clouds presaging a violent storm

BLACKBIRDER: a ship or person involved in the quasi-legal and illegal procurement of labourers for the Queensland canefields in the late 19th century

BLANKET/TARPAULIN MUSTER: fundraising; at a public event, a taut blanket is carried around the arena and people throw money on to it

BLIND FREDDIE [COULD SEE IT]: stating the obvious, used derisively

BLOCKY: an orchardist or grape grower on irrigated country, particularly along the Murray–Darling river system

B

BLOKE: a man

BLOODY: used as a superlative; with "hell" to express surprise; to extend a word or phrase and render it sardonic "Hoo-bloody-ray, three cheers for the Guv'nor-bloody-Gen'ral"; to add emphasis "This bloody job is no bloody good so I'll be bloody-well snatchin' it to-bloody-morrer"

BLOW: brag, boast; spend all one's money

BLOWHARD: boastful person, a braggart

BLOWIE: a blowfly

BLUDGE: to shirk one's responsibility, to live off others, to impose on

BLUDGER: one who bludges, formerly a bag swinger's pimp

BLUE (USED AS BOTH NOUN AND VERB): a mistake, "I made a blue"; a fight, an argument; red hair; blue roan is an attractive colour sometimes seen in cattle, particularly Illawarra Shorthorns

B

BLUE HEELER: an Australian cattle dog; a policeman

BLUE-CLAW: see *yabbie*

BLUEY: a common nickname for a red-haired person; a court summons

BOATIE: someone who messes about in boats

BOBBY DAZZLER: something outstanding

BODGIE: makeshift, unreliable. From the name of a teenage cult of the 1950s

BOGAN: a lout, uncultured person (derogatory and often offensive to many)

BOGAN SHOWER: two raindrops and a cloud of dust

B

BOGGI*: a type of large lizard, an early type of shearers' handpiece

BOGONG*: a moth that migrates in millions to the Australian Alps from the northern inland each summer

BOMMIE*: a reef or submerged rock where surf breaks

BONZER: really outstanding

BOOF: a yokel

BOOKIE: a bookmaker, SP— an unlicensed bookmaker. SP is "starting price" and all bets are paid out on the official starting price of the horse

BOOMER: a large male kangaroo

BOOMERANG*: an Aboriginal weapon; anything loaned that must be returned "Yeah, you can borrow me wheelbarrer, but she's a boomerang, mate."

BOONDIE (ALSO COONDIE)*: a stone

BOOZE BUS: police vehicle used for random breath testing

BORED, PUNCHED OR COUNTERSUNK, DON'T KNOW IF I'M: utterly confused

BOSHTER: excellent, top notch

BOSS COCKY: employer

BOTANY BAY HORNPIPE: the death throes of a convict hanged on the gallows

BOTANY BAY STRAWS: a grizzly lottery to escape the convict chain gangs. Three men would draw straws, the winner would kill the other two, knowing he was certain to be hanged.

BOTTLE SHOP: liquor store

BOTTLE-O: a liquor store; formerly a collector of bottles for recycling

BOTTLEBRUSH: vividly flowering shrubs or small trees of the Callistemon genus

B

BOURKE: an outback town in NSW, *back of Bourke* (beyond) is the mythical great emptiness, a simile for the limits of civilisation, also the legendary place of no work, see *Tallarook*

BOWERBIRD: a hoarder

BREKKIE: breakfast

BRIDGE, THE: Sydney Harbour Bridge

BRIEF: a lawyer

BRISBANITE: someone who lives in Brisbane

BROWN BOMBER: a parking warden

BRUMBY: a wild horse

BUCKLEY'S: no chance, in full "You have two

B

chances, Buckley's and Nunn", from a former Melbourne department store

BUDGIE: budgerigar [parakeet in the US]

BUDGIE SMUGGLERS: brief swimming trunks or underpants, the genital bulge reminiscent of bird smugglers. Wildlife smuggling is a serious offence in Australia and smugglers try all sorts of lurks to avoid detection.

BUGGER: like bastard, used in a multitude of ways

BUGGER IT: I don't care

BUGGER OFF: go away or leave

BUGGER-UP FINISH: dead

BUGGERED: ruined, broken, tired

BUGGERED OFF: disappeared

BUGGERS ON THE COALS: small johnny cakes, often sweetened with sultanas

BUGLE: on the nose, smelly

B

BULLOCKY: in former
times a bullock
(oxen) team driver
BULLSHIT MERCHANT:
car/insurance
salesperson, politician,
habitual liar

BUMBOY: an ill-paid and
often abused assistant
BUNDIE: Bundaberg Rum
BUNG*: broken,
infected "I've got a
bung eye"; dead
BUNNY: a scapegoat
BUNYIP*: a mythical
creature of the billabongs
BURLEY: food thrown
into the water to attract
fish; (US *chum*)
BUSH, THE: anywhere
away from the city,
the bush has achieved
almost mythical
status and is often

B

invoked by politicians at election time

BUSH BAPTIST: someone of no particular religion

BUSH FLY: the bane of southern Australian summers, a small black fly blown from the northern outback by prevailing summer winds

BUSH WEEK: legendary time when country folk visit the city, "Whadd'ya think it is, bush week?" is still used to berate a slow driver

BUSHFIRE: a dangerous and regular weather event of Australia, fierce forest fires fuelled to an awesome intensity by eucalypt oil

BUSHFIRE BRIGADE: country fire brigades, many of them voluntary

BUSHFIRE SEASON: late summer, though increasingly beginning much earlier

BUSHRANGER: highwayman

BUTCHER : once a 6-ounce beer glass (mainly SA)

CABBAGE PATCHER/ GUMSUCKER: Victorian

C

CABBAGE TREE: a type of palm, a hat made from the leaves was once the height of fashion

CALL FOR BERT: vomit

CAMP AS A ROW OF TENTS: very affected in manner

CAMP OVEN: a cast iron pot with a slightly concave, tight-fitting lid used as a versatile container for cooking meals in the ashes of a campfire

CARDY: cardigan

CARK IT: die

CASH IT IN: die

CASHED HIS CHEQUE: died

CAT-HEAD: [Eastern states]: see *double-gee*

CENTRE, THE: Central Australia, also Red Centre, Dead Heart

CHALKIE: a schoolteacher

CHATEAU CARDBOARD: wine sold in a foil bladder packed in a box

CHESTY BOND: a white singlet, named for the cartoon character advertising the brand

CHEW AND SPEW: takeaway food

CHIAK/SHIAK: tease, poke fun at, taunt

C

CHINAMAN: an improvised loading ramp
CHOOK: a chicken
CHRISSIE: Christmas
CHUCK: to throw, vomit; see *go*

CHUCK A DEEPY: go into a violent tantrum, sulk, an outburst of temper
CHUNDER: vomit
CIRCLE WORK: driving competitions for beaut utes, often an adjunct to B&S balls
CLAP STICKS: rhythm sticks used in Indigenous music
CLEANSKIN: in the pastoral industry an unbranded cattle beast; an unlabelled bottle of wine
CLINER: wife or steady girlfriend

C

CLOBBER: clothes

CLONCURRY SANDWICH: a billy goat between two bags of flour

CLOTHES HOIST: see *Hill's Hoist*

CLUCKY [CHOOK OR WOMAN]: broody, maternal

COATHANGER, THE: see *Bridge*

COBBER: a friend

COBBLER: in many trades an unpopular or difficult job [left to the last]

COBBLERS' PEGS: a wild marigold with small, sharp seeds that penetrate socks and clothing

COCK-EYED BOB: a cyclone

COCKATOO: a lookout, especially during illegal activities

C

COCKROACH: A New South Welshman (mostly used in the context of rugby league)

COCKY: cockatoo (the bird); formerly a small farmer but now applied to most farmers other than large landholders

> **COW COCKY:** dairy farmer
>
> **SHEEP COCKY:** wool producer
>
> **WHEAT COCKY:** grain grower

COCKY'S JOY: golden syrup (a light molasses)

CODGER: male, usually older

COLDIE: a beer

COLLINS STREET COCKY: a city professional who owns a vineyard or other genteel agricultural enterprise as a tax haven

COLONIAL GOOSE: rolled mutton flap stuffed with bread, herbs and seasoning

COME DOWN THE LADDER: see *get off your bike*

C

COME THE: try to put something over someone, or to act like something one is not, "— on", "— Queen of Sheba"

TO COME THE RAW PRAWN: try to hoodwink someone

COMPO: worker's compensation, paid sick leave granted as a result of accident or injury on the job

CONDUCTOR: road-train truckie

COO-EE: a penetrating call that carries over distance in the bush; in—: within earshot

COOLIBAH: a type of eucalypt that grows on flood-prone land

COP IT SWEET: accept one's fate

COP THE CROW: get the worst of a deal

CORNSTALKER: someone from New South Wales

CORROBOREE*: Indigenous ceremony, a party

COULD EAT THE LEG OFF A SKINNY PRIEST: very hungry

C

COULDN'T HIT A COW IN THE ARSE WITH A HANDFUL OF WHEAT: a poor shot or kick at goal, inaccurate

COULDN'T KNOCK/PULL THE SKIN OFF A RICE PUDDING: weak, lacking power (of a vehicle)

COUNTER LUNCH: a meal served at hotel bars

COUNTRY*: one's ancestral home

COVE: a man, suspicious character

COWBOY: slapdash, gerry builder, incompetent or unqualified tradie; a person, usually older, on a large grazing property who looks after the house cow and vegetable garden

CRACK: to achieve something [crack the lottery]; to solve, accomplish

CRACK A COLDIE: open a beer

CRACK IT HARDY: endure adverse conditions

CRANKY: in a bad mood

C

CRAWLER: someone who curries favour with those in authority; teacher's pet; boss's favourite

CRAYFISH: an uncoordinated person, a politician

CROOK: unwell, not quite right, unfair

CROOKED ON: to be angry with someone

CROSS-COUNTRY BUM-SNIFFING: rugby

CROWEATER: a South Australian

CROWN OF THORNS: a starfish that causes great damage on the Great Barrier Reef

CRUEL: to ruin something, spoil an opportunity

CRUET: the head

CRUST: one's income, "What do you do for a crust?"

CUNNING AS A DUNNY RAT: a slippery customer

CUP, THE: the Melbourne Cup, Australia's world famous horse race

CUPPA: cup of tea or, more lately, coffee

CYCLONE: hurricane, typhoon

D

DAGGY: unfashionable, untidy

DAKS: trousers; trackie—: tracksuit pants; under—: underpants

DAMPER: soda bread cooked in a camp oven

DARLING FLEA: a small, very sharp burr found on the Darling River floodplain

DARWINIAN: someone who lives in Darwin

DATE: anus

DATE ROLL: toilet paper

DAWN SERVICE: Anzac Day service to honour the war dead

DEAD MARINE: empty beer bottle. It may have its roots in the licence once issued to bottle-os, which stated they were "licensed marine collectors", a reference to jetsam washed ashore

DEAD SET: fair dinkum, absolute, no question about it, without doubt

DEADLY*: awe-inspiring, excellent, exciting, enviable, fashionable

C

DECKIE: a deckhand on a fishing boat

DEMON (ALSO DEE): detective

DERRO: a homeless alcoholic

DESERT, THE: inland Australia

DESERT VARNISH: oxidisation on stone surfaces in arid regions

DEVIL'S EYE: egg placed in a hole cut in a slice of bread and fried

DIAL: the face

DICKLESS TRACY: a policewoman

DIEHARD: someone set in their ways

DIGGER, DIG: member of the Australian armed forces, also used in addressing a close friend

DIKE: a communal lavatory

DILL: a fool

DILLY BAG*: a small woven bag used by Aboriginal people, now applied to any type of bag from a small backpack to a purse

DING: a softening of the offensive 'dago'; a scratch or dent

D

DINGBATS, IN THE: to have delirium tremens
DINK: to carry a passenger on a pushbike or motorbike
DINKUM: true, genuine, honest
DINKY DI: see *dinkum*
DINNER: lunch
DINNYHAZER: a knockout blow, used to denote something violent, e.g. a storm
DIP OUT: withdraw, miss out on something
DO: an action, often forceful; act like, "Do the Sydney toff"; a party
DOB IN: tell tales, inform on someone
DOBBER: a tattle tale
DOER: a character, usually in conjunction with an adjective, e.g "hard doer"
DOG ON THE TUCKERBOX: a statue outside Gundagai, NSW, a memorial to the bullock

D

teams. It derives from an anonymous poem with the refrain "And the dog shat in the tuckerbox, nine miles from Gundagai". The bowdlerised version has the dog sitting on the tuckerbox.

DOG: a police informer

DOG'S DISEASE: the flu, a cold

DOGGO, LIE: stay hidden, lie quietly, wait for something to pass

DOING A BOBBY LIMB: rising very early; Bobby Limb and his wife Dawn Lake were popular radio and TV personalities from the '50s to the '70s and the schoolboy joke went: "Why does Bobby Limb wake up early?" "He likes to get up at the crack of Dawn."

DOLE, THE: welfare payment to the unemployed

DOLE BLUDGER: a welfare cheat

DONGA: workers' accommodation at a mine or other remote site

DONK: a car or boat engine

D

DONKEY'S YEARS: a very long time, "I haven't seen her in donkey's years"

DOOLAN: a Catholic, also left-footer

DORK: clumsy, inept person

DO A [NELLIE] MELBA: repeatedly come out of retirement

DO A PERISH: die by misadventure

DO THE BLOCK: lose one's temper

DOUBLE-GEE: a spiked seed case, painful to step on (WA)

DOWN PAT: known by rote

DREAMING, THE/ DREAMTIME*: the long ago when the Earth and its denizens were created and the laws that govern them put in place

DRESSED UP LIKE A POX-DOCTOR'S CLERK: flashily dressed

DRESSED UP LIKE A SORE THUMB: in one's best clothes

DRONGO: a fool, dull-witted, ungainly

DROVER: someone who drives cattle or sheep over long distances

D

DRYBLOWER: a machine for separating metal from crushed ore using air rather than water, *see also yandy*

DUCK-SHOVE: to act unethically, to pass the buck

DUCK'S DINNER: drinking without eating

DUFFER: a counterfeiter or dealer in counterfeit goods, a livestock thief

DUMPER: a wave with a dangerous break, *see mine*

DUNNY: toilet, wc, bathroom, lavatory;

— budgie: blowfly

DURRIE: a cigarette

///

EAR-BASHER: an incessant talker

EASTERLY (WA): scorching dry winds that in summer blow off the deserts, sometimes for days

EASY BEATS: a team easily defeated (from the name of the pop group)

EMPTIES: the aftermath of a party [empty bottles]

F

EMU PARADE: group of volunteers collecting litter after an event
ESKY: an insulated cooler, from the name of a best-selling brand
EXY: expensive

FACE-ACHE: irritating or ugly person
FACE LIKE THE NORTH END OF A SOUTH-BOUND CAMEL: ugly
FAIR: used to add emphasis

FAIR COW: something not good
FAIR CRACK OF THE WHIP: take it easy, give me a chance, give me time
FAIR GO: to be treated equally with others, to give a sporting chance

D

FAN-TAN: a gambling game introduced by the Chinese during the gold rush and once very popular, though illegal

FANG: speed, push the accelerator to the floor

FANG FARRIER: a dentist

FANG/S: the teeth

FARTSACK: a sleeping bag

FATHER CHRISTMAS: Santa Claus

FELLER: a man

FERAL: a domesticated animal gone wild, a hippy, young sometimes vagrant people living in the subtropical hinterland

FILTHY: very good

FISHO: a fishmonger, someone who works in a fish and chip shop

FIZZGIG: a police informer

FLAKE: the shark meat used in fish and chips

FLASH: showy, ostentatious

FLASH AS A RAT WITH A GOLD TOOTH: ostentatious, showy, overdressed, gaudy

FLAT: an apartment

FLAT CHAT: very busy

FLAT OUT: very fast

F

FLATHEAD: a sea-fish, popular as a table fish

FLOATER: (SA) a meat pie in a bed of mushy green peas

FLYING DOCTOR: aircraft-borne outback medical service, brainchild of the Rev. John Flynn

FLYING FOX: a large fruit bat commonly seen in east-coast cities

FOOTY: Australian Rules Football

FOUREX: a Queensland beer

FOURPENNY DARK: cheap port wine

FRANGER: condom

FRED NERK: an imaginary person used as a scapegoat

FREMANTLE/ALBANY/ESPERANCE DOCTOR: strong, sea breezes that bring relief from scorching summer afternoons (WA)

FRESHIE: fresh-water crocodile

FRONT: effrontery, gall

FUNNEL-WEB: an extremely poisonous spider

F

FURPHY: a rumour, often spread deliberately

GALAH*: the roseate cockatoo, a silly person; ---session: gossip, time set aside for outback women to chat in the days when the only communication was by radio transmission

GALLOPS, THE: horse races

GAME: ready to try anything, brave; --- as Ned Kelly: very daring

GANDER: look at, investigate

GARBO: a refuse collector

GARGLE: to drink to excess

G

GEEK: look at, peer at

GENTLE ANNIE: a ferocious burr found in the irrigated country along the Murray–Darling river system, also a name given to numerous stretches of rising road throughout Australia

GET OFF YOUR BIKE: react violently to a suggestion or comment, "All right mate, don't get off your bike"

GET ONE'S ARSE INTO GEAR: spring into action

GET ON [MY] GOAT: be annoyed by someone

GET THE ROUGH END OF THE PINEAPPLE, TO: a raw deal, to be duped

GHAN: formerly a camel driver brought to Australia in the late 19th century by the government and large pastoralists, mainly from north-western India; The Ghan: the train that runs through Central Australia to Darwin

G

GHOST: from 'Holy Ghost', an exclamation of surprise
GIBBER*: a stone
GIBBER PLAIN/DESERT: country covered in tightly packed stones
GIDJI*: a spear (WA), an outback tree
GILGAI*: a waterhole (NSW)
GILGIE*: small freshwater crayfish (WA)
GING: a slingshot (WA, Qld)
GIVE 'EM CURRY: deal with severely

GIVE 'EM HEAPS: give no quarter
GIVE IT A BASH/BURL/FLY: to try, attempt
GIVE LARRY DOOLEY, TO: punishment, criticise harshly
GIVE THE POT AWAY: to tattle, to divulge a secret
GLOBE: a light bulb
GO BERKO: fly off the handle,
GO/GONE BUSH: left for the country, disappeared
GO BUTCHER'S: to berate someone, see *rhyming slang, crook*

G

GO CROOK AT/ABOUT:
complain, berate
GO DOWN THE MINE:
to be dumped by a
dangerous wave
GO FERAL: depart
from one's usual
behaviour or lifestyle
GO FOR THE DOCTOR:
call it quits
GO FOR YOUR LIFE: feel
free [to do something],
an expression of
encouragement
GO THE: to perform
some action, particu-
larly in sport, e.g.

"Go the biff" punch
an opposing player
GOD-BOTHERER: a priest
GOLDEN MILE:
Kalgoorlie, WA
GOLDFIELDS, THE: typically
refers to the area around
Kalgoorlie, WA
GOLLY: to spit
**[GOODBYE AND] THANK
YOUR MOTHER FOR THE
RABBITS:** a hurried
farewell, from the
punchline of a very
old, risqué joke
GONE WALKABOUT*: absent
from the usual haunts,

G

originally referring to the Aboriginal custom of travelling to special places for secret ceremonies

GOOD SORT: an agreeable person, usually referring to women

GOOG: egg, foolish person

GOOLY: phlegm, testicle

GOT THE WOBBLY BOOT ON: drunk

GOVERNMENT STROKE: to work very slowly

GRAB SOME ZEDS: sleep, nap

GRAFT: hard work

GRAUNCH/GRUNGE: a narrow opening

GRAZIER: a station owner or pastoralist

GREAT AUSTRALIAN ADJECTIVE, THE: see *bloody*

GREENGROCER: a fruit and vegetable seller

GREENIE: an environmentalist; someone on the left politically

G

GREY GHOST: a parking officer

GROG: once rum but now applies to any alcoholic drink

GROT, THE: any illness or disease

GRUNGY/GUNGEY: see *scungy*

GUBBA*: white person

GUERNSEY: the jumper worn by Australian Rules footballers; to get a—: to receive an award, be mentioned, run a place in a competition

GULF, THE: the Gulf of Carpentaria

GULLY-RAKER: once a cattle duffer, now a violent downpour

GUM: can refer to almost any tree in the eucalypt family, though usually reserved for smooth-barked types

GUN: someone very skilled at something, e.g. a gun driver

GUTSER: a heavy fall

GYNIE: gynaecologist

H

HAIRYMAN*: any one of many legendary man-like creatures in various parts of Australia of which the yowie is perhaps the most famous

HALF-ARSED: half-hearted
HALF-PIED: unfinished, crossbred, a poor imitation, not very useful
HAMMER: the back, heard in "Get off my hammer!" and often yelled at a tailgating driver
HAPPY AS LARRY: very happy, satisfied
HATTER: an eccentric, often a hermit [from *Alice in Wonderland*]
HAVE A BLOODY GO: expression deriding someone thought not to be trying

HAVE A GINK: a close look
HAVING A BAD TROT:
a run of bad luck
HEAD: one's physical
appearance

HEAD LIKE A BOARDING HOUSE/RAILWAY CUP OF TEA: big and weak
HEAD LIKE A ROBBER'S DOG: a furtive expression
HEAD, ROUGH: bordering on the ugly

HEAD SERANG: the boss
HEAPS: a large amount
or number
HEXHAM GREY: a large
and ferocious mozzie
from the swamps around
Hexham, NSW
HILL'S HOIST: a rotary
clothes line synonymous
with suburban Australia

H

HOBARTIAN/BARRACOUTER: a resident of Tasmania's capital
HOME AND HOSED: completed with time, money, etc. to spare
HOOF IT: to walk
HOOLY: a party
HOOLY/HOLY DOOLY: an exclamation of surprise
HOON: a lair; person, usually male, addicted to street racing; a dangerous driver
HOOP: a jockey
HORRORS, THE: delirium tremens, a bad hangover

HOSTIE: a flight attendant (from air hostess)
HOUSE GROUSE: the house wine in a restaurant

HOW ARE YOU POPPIN' UP: a greeting

HUEY: the god of rain and thunderstorms, in recent years also the god of surf. A thunderstorm on a hot summer's day will evoke cries of "Send 'er down Huey!"

HUMP: carry a heavy load

HUMPY*: a rough shelter, a hovel

HYDRAULICS: a popular nickname for a thief who'll 'lift anything'

ICING: a covering or topping of sweet paste on a cake (frosting in the USA)

IN LIKE FLYNN: to seize an opportunity, especially in regard to a sexual encounter (from actor Errol Flynn)

INSIDE COUNTRY: the antonym of outback, the closely settled country along the coast and hinterland

IN THE GUTS: the centre, the middle

IN THE NUDDY: naked

J

JACK OF IT: fed up

JACK UP: balk, refuse to carry out an order, dig in the heels

JACKAROO: male trainee station manager, see *jillaroo*

JACKIE HOWE: formerly a sleeveless woollen shirt, now a black or navy singlet

JAFFLE: a pie-like toasted sandwich made in a jaffle iron over an open flame

JARMIES: pyjamas

JESUS CHRIST: an expression of surprise, frustration, anger or derision

JESUS HILTON, THE: St Vincent's Private Hospital in Sydney

JILLAROO: female trainee station manager

JIMMY WOODSER: someone who drinks alone in a bar

JOE BLOW: John Citizen, Everyman

JOHNNY CAKES: small flat breads baked on the ashes

JOKER: a man

JUMBUCK: an old name for a sheep

JUMP-ABOUT: cheap wine, methylated spirits
JUMPER: a sweater
JUNGLE JUICE: any cheap or home-made liquor

KANAKA COMPANY, THE: Burns Philp and Company, once heavily involved in blackbirding
KANAKA*: descendant of indentured labourers removed from Melanesia to work in the canefields, see blackbirder; can be offensive but not when used in a political sense
KANGAROOS IN THE TOP PADDOCK: mentally disturbed
KEEP NIT: keep a lookout, stand watch
KELLY: an axe
KELPIE: the legendary Australian sheep dog

K

KICK IN: contribute to a cause
KICK-IT-WITH-YOUR-HEAD: soccer
KICK: pocket
KIMBERLEY SANDWICH: a goanna between two sheets of bark
KINDER/KINDIE: kindergarten
KIP: a flat piece of wood used in the game of two-up
KIWI: a New Zealander
KNOCK-ABOUT: earthy, down to earth, of the common folk

KNOCK-BACK: a refusal
KNOCKER: a constant critic
KNOCKING SHOP: brothel
KOORI*: (SE Australia): generic and political, an Aboriginal person
KYBOSH: to spoil, ban, to prohibit something is to put the kybosh on it
KYLIE*: (WA) boomerang

L

LAIR: a show-off, an ostentatious person

LAIRISE: to show off; to flaunt wealth or possessions

LAMBED DOWN: bankrupt, an itinerant worker who has been duped to spend all his money on booze

LAMINGTON: squares of sponge cake dipped in chocolate icing and shredded coconut

LARRIKIN: formerly a gang member, now usually a mischievous person

LASHING OUT: profligate spending

LAUGHING GEAR: the mouth

LEAGUE: Rugby League

LEG-OPENER: alcohol, particularly sparkling wine

LEMON SQUASH: lemon juice, often with the pulp, water and sugar

LEMONADE: a clear, carbonated soft drink, allegedly of lemon flavor

LICENSEE: publican

L

LIFT: an elevator
LIFT, TO: steal or purloin
LIGHT-ON: short measure, lacking in detail
LIKE A BLUE-ARSED FLY: rushing aimlessly about
LIKE A BUTCHER'S PICNIC: noisy, chaotic
LIKE A PORK CHOP [IN A SYNAGOGUE]: bewildered, agitated, unwanted, unpopular
LIKE A SHAG ON A ROCK: exposed, deserted, left to one's own devices
LIKE A STUNNED MULLET: dumbstruck

LIKE A TWO-BOB WATCH: erratic, unreliable
LIKE THE BUTCHER'S DOG: over-fed, butt of abuse, overweight
LIKE THE DROVER'S DOG: lean, 'all ribs and dick', hungry, ambitious, shown only grudging respect, butt of abuse
LIPPIE: lipstick
LITTLE BIT LONG TIME*: not yesterday but not all that long ago
LITTLE BIT LONG WAY*: not just down the road but not too far away

L

LOB: to arrive unexpectedly "The rellies lobbed in on me"
LOLLY: candy, confectionery
LOLLY, DO THE: lose one's temper

LOLLY WATER: any soft drink
LONDON TO A BRICK ON: very short odds
LONG PADDOCK: government droving routes along which sheep or cattle are driven, these days mainly in times of drought
LONG SOUP/SHORT SOUP: Australian Chinese clear chicken and vegetable soup with and without noodles respectively
LOONY FRIGHTENER: a psychiatric nurse

L

LORD/LADY MUCK [OF THE CHOOKHOUSE]: a pretentious person

LUMBERED: caught in the act, arrested, imprisoned
LUMPER: a dock worker (WA)

LUNATIC SOUP: alcohol, particularly cheap wine and spirits
LURK: something illegal or underhand, a racket, snide

MAD AS A CUT SNAKE: insane
MAD AS A MEAT AXE: very angry
MAG: to talk on and on, incessantly
MAGGOT: an umpire in Australian Rules Football

M

MAINLAND, THE:
Tasmanian name for
continental Australia
MAKE A QUID:
earn a living
MAKINGS, THE: tobacco
and cigarette papers
MALARKEY: foolish talk
MALLEE, THE: the
wheatbelt of WA and
parts of Vic. [from a
type of small tree]
MALLEE GATE: a makeshift
gate in a farm fence
MANCHESTER: cotton
goods such as sheets
and pillowcases

MAP OF TASMANIA/TASSIE:
a woman's pubic area
MARK: in Australian
Rules Football to catch
the ball on the full
MARRON*: a freshwa-
ter crayfish prized
for its flesh (WA)
MARY DRESS*: dresses
of colourful floral
print cloth favoured
by the women of the
Torres Strait Islands
MATE'S RATES: discount
given to a friend or
special customer
MATILDA: a swag

M

MEAT WORKS: an abattoir

MELBURNIAN: a resident of Melbourne

MEN'S BUSINESS*: ceremonies sacred to men

MIDDY: a small glass of beer, varying in size from state to state, see *schooner, pot*

MILKO: a person who delivers milk to the home

MISERABLE AS A BANDICOOT ON A BURNT RIDGE: very unhappy

MOB: a large number of anything

MOB-HANDED: joint action

MOCKER: clothes

MOCKERS: to spoil something, a jinx, "Don't put the mockers on me"

MONGER: greengrocer, fish shop owner, street vendor

MONGER, MUNJER: food

MONTY: a sure thing, a safe bet

MOOLAH: money

MOOSH: mouth

MORAL, A: in sports a certain winner

MORE ARSE THAN JESSE [THE COW]: extremely lucky

M

**MORE COMEBACKS
THAN LAZARUS:** said of
politicians who have a
career of ups and downs
**MORE FRONT THAN
MYERS:** extremely
audacious, Myer is a
large department store
**MORE THAN YOU COULD
POKE A STICK AT:** more
than one could possibly
want, overwhelmed
by numbers
MOSCOW: a pawnshop
MOTZA: a large
gambling win
MOZZIE: mosquito

MUD PIRATE: in former
times the men who
crewed the paddle
steamers on the Murray–
Darling river system
MUG: a foolish or incompetent person, the face
MUG LAIR: an offensive
show-off; someone
not worth the time
of day; see *lair*

M

MULGA, THE: the outback [from a type of small tree]

MULGA WIRE: bush telegraph

MULLET: hairstyle, short at the sides, long at back and top

MULLOCK HEAP: a mine's waste dump

MURPHIES: potatoes

MURRAY CRAY: freshwater crayfish (NSW, VIC)

MUSHIE: mushroom

MUSO: a musician

MUSTER: livestock round-up

MUTTONBIRD: various shearwaters, mainly the short-tailed, used as food

MY WORD: definitely

///////////////////////////////////////

NANA [BANANA]: head; do the—-: lose one's temper

NARK: a parking officer, a tell tale, a killjoy

NARKY: short-tempered

NED KELLY: legendary bushranger

NEVER-NEVER: the remotest outback

N

NEW AUSTRALIAN: a term coined by government in the 1950s to describe European immigrants other than the English

NEW CHUM: newly arrived immigrant

NICK: state of fitness or condition

NICK OFF: to leave suddenly

NIGGLY: grumpy; testy

NINETY CENTS IN THE DOLLAR: not all there, a simpleton

NIPPER: a child

NIPPON CLIP-ON: extra transit lanes designed by a Japanese firm and added to the Sydney Harbour Bridge

NOB: a self-important person, the boss

NO GOOD TO GUNDY: useless

NO-HOPER: someone incapable of redemption

NONG: slow-witted person

NOONGA*: generic and political, an Aboriginal person (SA)

NO WORRIES: see *no sweat*

NOR-WESTER: hot, summer winds (eastern states)

NO SWEAT: easily done or accomplished, don't worry

N

NOT AS GREEN AS I AM CABBAGE-LOOKING:
not as silly as I look, not easily fooled
NOT IN A BULL'S ROAR:
a long way away
NOT THE FULL QUID: not all there, a simpleton
NOVOCASTRIAN: a resident of Newcastle, NSW
NULLA-NULLA*: a club
NURSE [A BABY]:
hold, comfort
NYUNGA/NOONGAR*:
generic and political, an Aboriginal person (south-west WA)

OCKER: uncultivated person, yobbo, bogan
OCKERINA: a female ocker
OCKY STRAP: elastic strap for securing light loads

OFFICE, THE: advice
OFFSIDER: an assistant
OLD-MAN: anything large and or notable, worthy of admiration, e.g. old-man gum tree, old-man eagle, old-man river
OLDIES: parents, older relatives
ON FOR YOUNG AND OLD: an all-in brawl, commotion
ON MY GINGER: close behind, "Right on my ginger"
ON THE KNOCKER: right on time

ON THE NOSE: suspicious, smelly
ON THE OFF [CHANCE]: perhaps, maybe, a chance of "I might go on the off that she'll be there"
ON THE PAD: walking quietly or creeping
ON THE TAKE: begging, accepting a bribe
ON THE TOE: a state of nervous anticipation
ON THE TOOTH: hungry
ON YA: exclamation of approval meaning "well done"
OOROO, OORAY: goodbye

O

OPERA HOUSE, THE:
Sydney Opera House,
the architectural
marvel designed by the
Dane, Jørn Utzon

OPEN SLATHER: a free
for all; anything goes

ORSTRALIEAH: Australia,
a sardonic rendering of
the upper-class English
pronunciation of the name

OUTBACK: the inland, the
country beyond closer
settlement; see *inside*

PACK-A-POO: a Chinese
lottery once popular
among the poor

PACKING 'EM: very afraid

PADDOCK: a farmer's
field, a football ground

PADDOCK BASHER:
decrepit vehicle used
for rough farm work

PAPERBARK: loose-
barked members of
the melaleuca genus

PASH: kiss

PASSIONKILLERS: pantyhose

PASTORALIST: a
station owner

PATTER: a salesman's spiel

P

PAV: pavlova, a meringue-based dessert
PENCILLER: a bookmaker's clerk
PERTHITE: someone living in Perth
PERVE: ogling the opposite sex
PICCANINNY DAYLIGHT: false dawn
PICK: to annoy, nag
PICKY: fussy
PICNIC RACES: outback horserace meetings
PIE-EATER: of a person, insignificant, small-time

PIG'S [ARSE]: to refute a statement
PIKER: a hesitant or cowardly person
PISS: alcohol, particularly beer; urinate
PISS ANT, A: foolhardy person
PISS OFF: leave now [derogatory]

P

PISSED: drunk
PISSED OFF: annoyed
PISSING AGAINST THE WIND:
attempting the
impossible
**PISS IN SOMEONE'S
POCKET:** to ingratiate
oneself, toady to

PITT STREET FARMER:
see *Collins Street cocky*
PLAY SILLY BUGGERS: putting
one over, try to trick
someone, acting the fool
PLONK: cheap wine
see *fourpenny dark,
red ned, jump-about*
PODDY CALF/LAMB:
one raised by
bottle feeding
PODDY DODGER:
cattle rustler
**POKE THE BORAK*/
MULLOCK:** deride,
belittle, insult
POKIES: poker machines

P

POM: specifically a person from England. It does not apply to the Welsh, Scots or Cornish
POMMYLAND: England
PONGO LAND: England
PONY: smallest beer glass
POOR BUGGER/SILLY BUGGER/BAD BUGGER: referring to people
PORT: briefcase, portmanteau, schoolbag
POSSIE: chosen position at an event

POSTIE: mailman, letter carrier
POT: the largest measure of beer glass
PRANG: auto or bicycle accident

P

PRETTY: almost, to some extent, "Pretty well finished", "Pretty good"

PRETTY SALLY: any one of various hills of this name throughout Australia

PREZZIE: gift

PRINCE ALBERTS: triangles of calico wrapped around the feet in place of socks and worn by outback workers

PROP: to pull up suddenly, to dig one's heels in

PUFTALOON: a kind of scone

PULL A SWIFTIE: sleight of hand, pull a fast one

PULLOVER: a jumper without buttons, sometimes sleeveless, pulled on over the head

PULL UP STUMPS: leave

PURLER: exceptional; fall off something: "I came a purler off the wall"

PUSHIE: a bicycle

PUSHING SHIT UP A HILL WITH A POINTED STICK: battling against the odds

PUT THE ACID ON: coerce, pressure, persuade with force

PUT THE COLD BITE ON: ask someone for money with no preliminary warning, beg

~~~~~~

QUEENSLANDER: a type of house raised on stilts eminently suited to the tropics

QUICK SMART: rapid, swift action

QUOIT: the anus, backside

R

RABBIT-PROOF FENCE:
any one of several
long mesh fences
constructed to prevent
wild rabbits from
entering pastoral areas
**RACE THAT STOPS
A NATION, THE:** the
Melbourne Cup
RACEHORSE: a very thin
hand-rolled cigarette
RACK OFF: go away
RAPT: overjoyed
RATBAG: a villain
RAT-TRAP: grilled open
sandwich of cheese
and Vegemite

RATTLER: once a slow
country train service,
now any passenger train
RATTLING THE CAGE:
taunting someone
to get a reaction
RAZOO/BRASS RAZOO: a
mythical coin of little
value, "Not worth
a brass razoo"
RECCY: to reconnoitre
RECKON: think, estimate
RECOVERY/SUFFERING, A:
a hangover
RED NED: cheap red
wine see *fourpenny
dark, jump-about*

R

REDBACK: a poisonous spider

REEF, THE: Great Barrier Reef

REGO: motor vehicle registration papers

RELLIES: relatives

RHYMING SLANG: using rhymed phrases to represent another word. Though hundreds are in use, many others are used only by the people who coined them and are not very imaginative and so only a few are mentioned here:

BARRY CROCKER: shocker, terrible

BILLY LID: a child (kid)

BUTCHER'S [HOOK]: unwell (crook)

CAPTAIN COOK: look

CHINA [PLATE]: mate, good friend

EAU DE COLOGNE: telephone

HAMMER [AND TACK]: back

KEMBLA [GRANGE]: loose/small change

R

MICKEY MOUSE [EXTRA GROUSE]: very good

NOBBY [CLARK]: former Governor of Reserve Bank, shark

OXFORD [SCHOLAR]: dollar

RUBBITY [DUB]: pub, a hotel

SEPPO [SEPTIC TANK]: Yank

TO AND FROM: Pom, Englishman

RIDGY DIDGE: the genuine article, the real McCoy

RIGHTO: okay, indicating acceptance

RING: to call on the telephone

RINGBARK: killing a tree by removing a strip of bark right around the trunk; girdling

RING-IN: an imposter, underhand substitution

RINGER: stockman, fastest shearer in a team

RIPPER: something really exciting

R

ROAD TRAIN: a series of large trailers (up to four) towed by a prime mover, sometimes with its own fixed tray
ROCK SPIDER: paedophile
ROLLIE: a hand-rolled cigarette
ROO: kangaroo

ROO-BAR: nudge bar on a vehicle
ROOT: sexual intercourse
ROOTED: exhausted
ROPEABLE: very annoyed, angry
RORT: a lurk, a swindle, abuse the system
ROTTEN: very drunk
ROUGH AS GUTS/ BAGS: crude
ROUSE: nag, berate
ROUSEABOUT/ROUSIE: general labourer, particularly in a shearing shed

R

[ROYAL] SHOW, THE:
Agricultural fairs held in
the State capitals, usually
abbreviated to the Royal
RSL: Returned Services
League, an association
founded to protect
the interest of war
veterans; the local club
RUN A DRUM: come
second or third
RYEBUCK: the
genuine article

SALTIE: the dangerous
estuarine crocodile

SALVO: a member of
the Salvation Army
SALVOS: the
Salvation Army
SAMBO: sandwich

SANDGROPER: West Australian

SANDHILL: a dune, coastal or inland

SANDY BLIGHT: any of various eye infections once common in the outback

SANGER: sandwich

SCHOOL: a group of gamblers or drinkers

SCHOOLIE: a just-finished high-school student

SCHOONER: a beer measure between middy and pot

SCUNGY: unsavoury, dirty, untidy

SEAGULL: a casually employed waterside worker

SELFIE: a self-portrait taken with a mobile phone

SEMI: a semi-trailer truck

SERVO: petrol station, gas station

SESSION: an extended period of drinking

SETTLERS ALARM CLOCK: the kookaburra

SHAG: sexual intercourse

S

SHAGGIN' WAGON: a panel van, often greatly modified
SHAKY ISLES: New Zealand
SHANDY: beer mixed with lemonade
SHANGHAI: a boys' catapult used for propelling stones, see *ging*
SHANGHAI CHICKEN: feral pigeon
SHANTY: an unlicensed grog shop

SHARK AND TATIES: fish and chips
SHE: a pronoun applied to any situation, object or event, "She was a ripper of a game"
SHE'LL BE RIGHT/APPLES/SWEET: everything will go well; everything is all right

SHE'S JAKE: everything is all right

SHEARER: one who shears sheep for a living

SHEARING SHED: large farm building where sheep are shorn

SHEET-SNIFFER: a welfare officer (a reference to investigations into whether couples are sharing a bed or just accommodation so that they are not paid the wrong allowance)

SHEILA: a woman or girl (not derogatory, though some people believe it to be so) from a popular Irish name

SHELLACKING: comprehensive defeat, whitewash

SHERRIN: the ball used in Australian Rules, its brand name

SHINY-ARSED: applied to some participants in recreational pursuits, particularly cyclists and surfers. Not serious, more interested in equipment and costume than the pursuit, e.g. Lycra-clad bicycle commuters

S

SHIRALEE: a swag
SHIVOO: a party
SHONKY: second rate
SHOOT THROUGH: depart in a hurry (originally "Shoot through like a Bondi tram[car]")
SHORT BACK AND SIDES: the universal men's hairstyle prior to the late 1950s
SHOT: reached one's limit of endurance, broken down, ruined
SHOUT: to buy a round of drinks

SHOW: mineral discovery; party; a war; likelihood of "They've got no show of winning this one"
SHRAPNEL: small change
SICKIE: taking a paid sick day when not ill
SING*: to put a curse on someone, to fulfill one's obligations to country by performing the appropriate rituals
SINGLET: a sleeveless undershirt
SINK THE FANGS, TO: a pressing request for a loan

SITTING UP LIKE JACKIE: proud, standing out in the crowd. This was once an offensive term, Jackie being an old generic name for a male Aboriginal. It referred to someone "aping his betters", an Aboriginal travelling in a horse and sulky for example, but time and usage have taken away its sting

SKERRICK: smallest amount, a fragment

SKIPPY: a jingoistic Australian; Coming the— exaggerating one's Australian-ness from a popular children's TV series *Skippy the Bush Kangaroo*

S

SKITE: to brag, show off
SKY PILOT: a clergyman
SLAB: a carton
of beer cans
**SLAP IN THE FACE WITH
A DEAD MULLET:** see
*better than a poke in the
eye with a burnt stick*

**SLAP IN THE FACE
WITH WARM LETTUCE:**
token punishment
SLASH: to urinate
SLAUGHT: an abattoir
SLING: to pay a
bribe or gratuity
SLIPPERY BOB:
fritters made from
flour, egg and
animal brains
SLUSHY: a cook's offsider
SLY GROG: liquor
sold illegally
SMOKE-OH/SMOKO:
a short rest break
during work periods

SMOODGE: to kiss, cuddle up to

SMOODGER: a sycophant

SMUG AS A RAT WITH AN UMBRELLA: very self satisfied

SNAFFLE: to purloin, unofficially commandeer

SNAGGER: an inexpert shearer

SNAGS: sausages

SNATCH IT/SNATCH ONE'S TIME: leave a job

SNERVE: see *franger*

SNIDE: illegal, of suspicious origin, crooked

SNOTTER: to hit or punch someone

SOCCER: what the rest of the world calls football

SOFT DRINK: non-alcoholic beverage, usually carbonated, e.g. dry ginger ale, US pop

SOL: shit on the liver, in a bad mood

SOOK: a sulky person, someone who is easily hurt or offended

SOOL ['EM]: a command to a dog to attack

S

SOU: small amount (of money), "I haven't got a sou"

SOUTHERLY BUSTER: on the east coast violent summer squalls that bring rain, hail and can lower the temperature by 10°C or more in minutes

SPAG BOL: spaghetti bolognaise

SPARROW STARVER: a street sweeper

SPARROW'S BREAKFAST: very little to eat [a shit, a drink of water and a good look round]

SPECCY: spectacular, in Australia Rules Football a high mark

SPELL: a rest, a work break

SPIDER: a soft drink with a scoop of ice-cream

SPIELER: a swindler, card shark

SPINE-BASHER: a lazy person

SPINE-BASHING: sleeping, a nap

SPIT THE DUMMY: to throw a tantrum, hence dummy spit. A dummy is known in America as a pacifier

SPORT: an affectionate form of address
SPROG: a baby
SPROGGY: sparrow
SPRUIKER: a barker, someone employed to attract custom

SQUARE AND LEMON: a drink of sarsaparilla and lemonade, sarsaparilla was once sold in square bottles (Tas)
SQUATTER: someone who occupies Crown Land -- at one time vast acreages -- with no legal title
SQUATTOCRACY: the Squatters as a political force, derisory term for large landholders who considered themselves members of an elite class
SQUIB IT: to run away from a challenge

S

SQUIZ: to peer at; an inquisitive look

STACK: an accident

STACK ON: to act vigorously; to stage, 'stack on a show'; theatrically lose one's temper

STANDING AROUND LIKE A STALE BOTTLE OF PISS: useless, unwanted

STAR BOARDER: a live-in lover, the relationship with whom is a poorly kept secret

STATION: vast sheep or cattle grazing property, measured in square kilometres, where livestock is grazed on the rangeland system

STATION HAND: general worker on a large pastoral property

STEAM: cheap wine, methylated spirits;

STEAM, LIKE: energetically, enthusiastically

STICKYBEAK: a nosy person, to pry or snoop

STIRRER: an agitator, troublemaker

STOCKMAN: a sheep or cattle station employee
STOKED: thrilled
STONE: starve
STONE/STARVE/STIFFEN THE CROWS: an expression of disgust
STOUSH: a disturbance, a fight or brawl

STREWTH: an exclamation of surprise or amazement
STRIDES: trousers
STRIKE ME PINK/PURPLE/ LUCKY: an exclamation of surprise
STRINE: Australian pronunciation satirised in a book written by 'Affabeck Lauder'
STROPPY: aggressive, defensive, feisty, in a state of agitation
STUBBIE: a 375mL beer bottle
STUBBIES: a type of shorts

S

STUFFED: exhausted, broken beyond repair
SUB: an advance on wages
SUBBY: a sub-contractor
SUCKED IN: deceived, tricked, swindled
SUNNIES: sunglasses
SURF BOAT: a whaler-like rowing boat once used in mass surf rescues, now only in competitions
SURF LIFE-SAVER: volunteer member of beach safety patrols, lifeguards

SUSS: suspect
SUSS OUT: reconnoitre
SUSSO, THE: social security; welfare money
SWAG: a bedding roll
SWAGMAN, SWAGGIE: an itinerant worker
SWY: see *two-up*
SYDNEYSIDER: a resident of Sydney

///

TAH: thank you
TAILOR-MADE: a factory-made cigarette
TAKE A SHOOFTY: investigate, look at

TAKING THE MICK[EY]: see piss, taking the

TAKING THE PISS: teasing, trying to dupe someone

TALLAROOK: a town in Victoria immortalised in the saying "things are crook in Tallarook"

TAR/BITUMEN, THE: sealed road; roads in closely settled areas

TASMANIAC: a Tasmanian

TASSIE: Tasmania

TASWEGIAN: Tasmanian

TEA: dinner

TEA-TREE: any one of various leptosper-mums, some of which have medicinal value

TECHNICOLOUR YAWN/ YODEL: vomit

TEE UP: arrange an event, organise

TEN-POUND POM: an assisted-passage English immigrant, often used derisively

T

TERRITORIAN: a resident of the Northern Territory

THINGS ARE CROOK IN TALLAROOK/THERE'S NO WORK IN BOURKE: see *Tallarook, Bourke*

THONGS: rubber sandal modelled on the Japanese getta, flip flops

TIGER FRIGHTENERS: jodphurs, polo players' breeches

TIN HORSE: small 4WD vehicle used to muster cattle

TINNIE: beer in a can; an aluminium dinghy or small boat

TINNY: flimsy, poorly made

TOEY: ready for action

TOMAHAWKER: a rough shearer who cuts the skin of the sheep too often

TOO EASY: see *no sweat*

TOO RIGHT: an expression of affirmation "It was a ripper of a game." "Too right, mate!"

TOORAK TRACTOR: an expensive 4WD such as a Range Rover, alluding to residents of wealthy suburbs who own farms or vineyards as tax havens

TOOTH: adjective describing an organisation known for well-catered meetings, e.g. "tooth Rotary"

TOP END, THE: the far north, particularly the East Kimberley/Northern Territory region

TRICK-ME: an imitation, "trick-me snags" vegetarian sausages

TROPICS, THE: north of the Tropic of Capricorn

TROPPO, GONE: insane, unhinged, a reference

T

to people affected by the monsoon season in the Top End

TROTS, THE: harness races; diarrhoea

TRUCKIE: a truck driver

TRUE BLUE: something genuinely Australian

TUCKER: food

TURN IT UP: stop doing that; stop trying to fool me, what do you take me for?

TURN UP FOR THE BOOKS: unexpected, (at a race meeting an unsatisfactory outcome for the bookmakers)

TURPS: cheap alcohol

TWO-POT SCREAMER: a noisy drunk, unable to tolerate liquor

TWO-UP: a gambling game played by tossing two pennies from a kip and gambling on whether they will fall heads or tails

---

UEY: u-turn, chuck a ---, perform a u-turn

UNDERGROUND MUTTON: wild rabbit

UP A GUM TREE: confused, in difficulties

UP THE DUFF: pregnant

UP TO PUSSY'S BOW: up to one's neck in something, fed up, exasperated

UP YOURS [FOR THE RENT]: to express disobedience; a refusal to cooperate

UPS, IN TWO: very soon

USEFUL AS A ROO-BAR ON A SKATEBOARD: utterly useless, superfluous, ostentatious

UTE: utility, a dual purpose light truck with a sedan cab, now also refers to the American-style pick-up truck

V

VB: Victoria Bitter, a beer
VEGEMITE: a tart, salty relish; happy little—: contented
VICTA: the original lawnmower with a rotary blade

WADDY*: a club
WAGGING: playing truant
WALLOPER: a policeman
WANKER: a fool (from wank: masturbate)
WARRIGAL GREENS: native spinach

WATTLE: any one of many golden-flowered trees or shrubs in the acacia family — the golden wattle is Australia's national flower
WHACKO: indicating approval
WHACKO THE DUCK/GOOSE/ CHOOK: used to applaud an action or statement
WHARFIE: a dock worker

WHEELIE: a wheelstand on a motorbike, circle work

WHEN JC/JESUS CHRIST PLAYED HALF-BACK FOR JERUSALEM: a long time ago; also, 'when JC wore short pants'

WHERE THE PELICAN FLIES: the far outback

WHINGEING POM: the archetypal English immigrant

WHINGER: a habitual complainer, the English in Australia are often accused of being whingers; see *Pom*

WHIP-ROUND: an impromptu collection for someone in financial trouble or any other cause

WHIPPER SNIPPER: weed whacker

WHITE ANT: termite

WHITE-ANT, TO: undermine another's efforts

WHITE LADY: methylated spirits

WHITE-SHOE BRIGADE: real estate developers

WIDEAWAKE HAT: a man's hat with no nap to the felt

WIDGIE: a female bodgie

WILLY WAGTAIL: a bird, a small and fearless flycatcher with endearing habits

WILLY-WILLY: a whirlwind, sometimes approaching tornado force

WINDCHEATER: sweatshirt

WISE MEN FROM THE EAST: people from the eastern states (WA)

WITCHETTY GRUB: a large edible grub found around the roots of certain shrubs (central Australia)

WOBBLY: a tantrum or angry outburst

WOG, THE: the flu, any malady; Mediterranean or Middle-Eastern immigrant, now rarely used and it has lost its sting among most people

WOMEN'S BUSINESS*: ceremonies sacred to women

WONGAI*: talk, discussion

X

WONKY: unstable, unsteady, dizzy

WOOLGROWER: a sheep cocky on a large scale; see *grazier, pastoralist*

WOOMERA*: a spear thrower, the weapons-testing site of the same name

WOOP-WOOP: mythical town a long way from anywhere

WORKING OFF A DEAD HORSE: working to repay a debt or for wages already paid

WOULDN'T GET A KICK IN A STREET-FIGHT: abuse yelled at a footballer having a bad day

WOWSER: a killjoy, a puritan

WURLEY*: a temporary shelter, a house, see *humpy*

XMAS: the form of Christmas incorporating the "Greek cross" or chi, often used in Australia

YABBER: talk incessantly, meaningless conversation

YABBER*: talk, conversation

YABBIE*: a freshwater crayfish, increasingly popular as restaurant fare

YACHTIE: a participant in yachting, cruising or racing

YAKKA*: work

YANDY*: to pan for tin or gold by winnowing crushed ore

YANKING THE CHAIN: see *rattling the cage*

YARDMAN: a hotel handyman

YARD-AND-A-HALF OF DIRTY PUMP WATER, A: a gangly youth

YARN: a story, tall or otherwise, to converse

YEO: old dialect for a ewe, heard in traditional songs (bare-bellied yeo)

YOBBO: rude person, a lout

YOU WOULDN'T READ ABOUT IT [IN PIX]: expressing incredulity

or disbelief (*Pix* was a
popular magazine of
the more lurid kind)
YOWIE*: a supernat-
ural being

ZAMBUK: a St John
Ambulance officer.
They once gave
first aid at sporting
events and were
nicknamed for a
proprietary
ointment
they carried
ZIFF: a beard

Frank Povah

Frank Povah's relationship with AUSTRALIAN GEOGRAPHIC began with the first issue in 1987, when he picked up a mistake missed by all others. He became an AG copy editor, a service he still renders today. Author of the long-running *Dinkum Lingo* column, Frank is one of the few true-blue Aussies whose love for Australia is matched by his encyclopaedic knowledge of its history, language and people.